Discovering

A Journey Book about adoption

by
Betsy Trainor

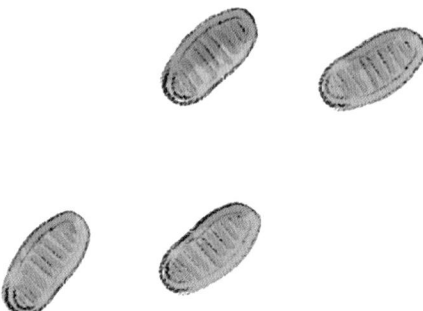

Every single baby in the world starts their journey with a birth family in a different way.

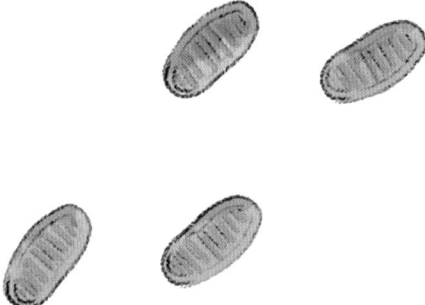

A birth family might be just a mommy or maybe a mommy, daddy, and other kids. There are too many different kinds of birth families to count.

Babies need a lot of things when they are born. They need a place to live where they can be protected, have food, and get plenty of love. Not every birth family can give a child all of those things at once so sometimes a plan is made to let a forever family help out.

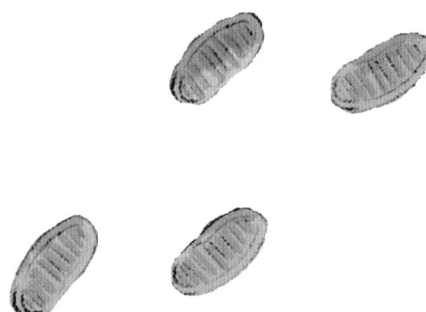

A plan to find a forever family could happen right away after a baby is born. Other times, it might not happen until the baby has grown into a toddler, or a big kid, or even a teenager. It just depends on what is best for everyone.

When a forever family brings home a child to stay with them, it is called an "adoption." It is a very exciting time because it is the beginning of a new family.

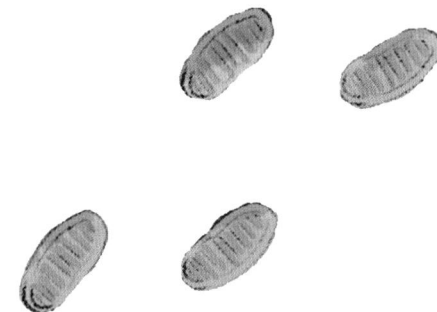

Forever families come in all different shapes, sizes, and colors. Some forever families all look like each other. Other forever families look very different from one another. It is fun to imagine who might grow up to be big and tall or who has curly hair or who has beautiful brown skin or who has a freckled face. It would be such a boring world if we were all the same.

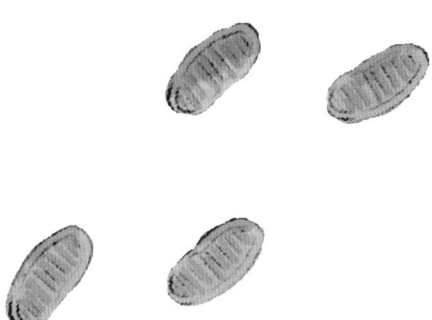

Being curious about your birth family can make you feel many different emotions. You might feel happy, sad, angry, or confused when you think about your own story.

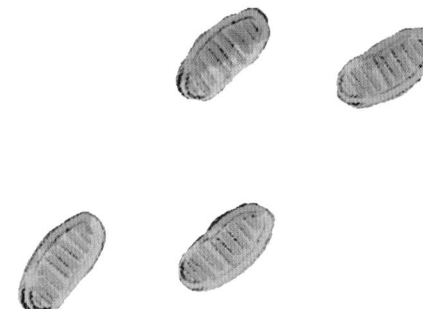

Some forever families might know a lot of different things about your birth family and others might not know very much at all. Talking to your forever family about your adoption can help you better understand your journey and answer some of the questions you are thinking about.

A nice thing to remember is that new forever families are created every day around the world. It is great to see so many people coming together to make all different types of families.

Throughout your life, you will meet many other people who have been adopted just like you. Each story is unique and very special.

Discovering how your journey began is the first piece of the puzzle that draws the picture of your life. Carry it close to your heart, and remember how very much you are loved!

The End

Made in the USA
Lexington, KY
30 June 2016